Cinders Rekindled:

Poems

By

Charlie R. Braxton

Jawara Press

Also by Charlie R. Braxton:

Ascension from the Ashes (1990)
Gangsta Gumbo (2012)

Published by Jawara Press
PO Box 2595
Jackson, MS 39207

Cover Art by Ms. Brenda Claiborne
Photos (Charlie Braxton and Cover Art) by Linus Morgan
Cover Design by Dub G

ISBN 978-0-9836527-0-0

Printed in the United States of America

Cover Art

The cover of this collection features the work of artist Brenda Claiborne, a native of Jackson, MS who is a renaissance woman and a survivor. The fourth daughter of an impoverished family of eight, she was raised by her grandmother with three of her siblings, and has endured the racism of Mississippi in the 50's and 60's, homelessness, a tumultuous family life, and cancer. These events in her life did not break her spirit; rather, they inspired her to seek refuge in her creativity.

Ms. Claiborne was the only one of her siblings to graduate from high school, college, and obtain a graduate degree. A graduate of Lanier High School, she worked in corporate America for 20 years before retiring to reevaluate her life. At the age of 40, she realized that business was not her calling and decided to pursue her dreams. She was inspired to create art when her daughter enrolled in art class and needed help. When both of her daughters were in college, she decided to enroll and pursue a degree in fine arts. She excelled in her coursework and graduated from Jackson State University with a Bachelors of Art in Art (2007) and completed a Master of Fine Arts at Mississippi College (2010). Ms. Claiborne currently resides in Ft. Washington, Maryland and more information may be found at www.brendaclaiborne.com.

Contents

Acknowledgements

First and foremost, I wish to acknowledge my ancestors whose spirits have guided and protected me throughout this journey we call life. Your strength, memory, wisdom and courage live through me, my children and their children to come:

Ms. Bonnie Bell Christopher, Maggie Braxton-Wallace, Kemp Braxton, Charlie Braxton (Dad), Lilly Braxton-Kline, Vernelle Braxton, Earl Kline, Elmer Otis, Willie "Jack" Ashley, Charles Junior Ashley, Elisabeth Cate, L.J. Martin, Leola Martin, Joe Martin, Jerry Martin, Larry Martin, Phillip Martin, Geneva Woodard, Robert June Woodard, J.L. Woodard, Julia Woods, Annie Lee Carroll, Diane Carroll, Michael Robinson, Virgie Brock-Shed, David Brian Williams, John Reese, John Otis Williams, Margaret Walker Alexander, Willie Cook and Carry Belton.

To my family whom I love more than life itself, thank you:

Mary L Woodard, Johnnie Robinson, Calvin Braxton, Hugh Earl Braxton, Kwame Braxton (thanks for suggesting the title, son), Hope Robinson, Kamau Braxton, Nzinga Braxton & Nile Braxton.

I also wish to acknowledge the following people for contributing significantly to my work:

Jerry Ward, Nayo Barbara Watkins, Kevin Powell, C. Liegh McInnis, Rosalie Daniels, Amiri Baraka, Sonia Sanchez, Ira Sullivan, Jabari Asim, Allen Gordon, Tony Medina, Kalamu ya Salaam, Sterling Plumpp, Nia Damali, Askia M. Toure, Kupenda Auset, John Michael Shaw, Carlton Wade, Timothy Washington, Harry Allen, Karen Goode, Curtis Austin, Rufus Mapp, Greg Jackson, Cassandra Wilson, Brian Ward, Ramona Ward, Cheo Coker, Al Young, Eugene B. Redmond, Alphonso Bailey, Alphonso Mayfield, Donnie Cross, Lenard D. Moore, E. Ethelbert Miller, Mariba Lumumba, Alvin Fielder, Ameen Rashid, Walter Liniger, Carlotta Abrams, Tommie "T-Bone" Pruitt, Vasti & Kathy Jackson, Brenda Claiborne, Preselfannie McDaniels, Linus Morgan and Dub G.

Introduction

Between Braxton's first book of poems, *Ascension from the Ashes* (1990), and this second volume is a lake of incineration, the space wherein the risen phoenix transforms cinders into embers and embers into flames of black fire (circa 1968) in order to burn the anger of redemption into American consciousness grown lazy and blind under the influence of "progress" or supersubtle fictions of social and political change. Those familiar with his earlier work, including his poems anthologized in *In the Tradition: An Anthology of Young Black Writers* (1992), *Bum Rush the Page* (2001) and *Role Call: A Generational Anthology of Social and Political Black Literature and Art* (2002), will note a shift from the lyric mode of "Bluesman" and the blues ethos of "We Can't Afford to Die" to a relentless riffing on the anger of feeling and the feeling of anger. Indeed, the poems in *Cinders Rekindled* are eruptive/disruptive proofs for the final lines of Braxton's poem "The Arts Are Black" ---

the bombs & bullets
hurled
from the suffering soul
of a real black artist.

What is of special importance is Braxton's refusal to discard the vocabulary and poetics associated with the

Black Arts/Black Aesthetic Movement either for the rhymes, inventions, and rhythms of spoken word or for the delicacies of craft and sensibility that are in stark contrast to the class-marked utterances of the neo-hip hop generation of poets. For he reminds us that we often have game in talking about suffering, but we only rarely want to hear the sound of suffering. His refusal, however, is not a signal of his being enslaved by the past but rather a sign that fidelity to poetry as polemic or political challenge remains a vibrant option. Given Braxton's transformations of allusions to old-time black religion into the militant anger of the unfinished revolutions in American human rights and human relations, one may tentatively conclude that he has bravely risked the aesthetics of the abrasive. The cumulative impact of Braxton's poetry may be an ironic transformation of readers into stalwart witnesses of the chaos that is now as it serves as a foil for continuing efforts to wring the sublime and the beautiful out of the vernacular.

As a poet, Braxton defies the premature comfort that may accompany change; his is the fierce preservation of traditions of the near past, an affirmation that genuine poetry involves tracing of a people's diverse states of being and thought. Braxton's work is an affirmation that the prophecy that lends power to the jeremiad burns productively in "the suffering soul/of a real black artist." Do not ask what is real. Feel what is audacious in the flames of anger as redemption.

Jerry W. Ward, Jr.
April 10, 2011

Part 1

Music is the Spark

Blues Lick #2

like the great spirit
of the holy ghost
on that right & mighty day
of pentecost
I come quick with a blues so smooth
it'll make you switch
from sittin' & broodin'
to sho' nuff movin' & groovin'
to my bubblin' brown suga shuffle
I say dance, dance, dance
to the rhythm I rip
wrapped in the sweet rock
of sacred ages
yeah I got poets,
scholars & sages
writin' books chapters
& pages
analyzin' the notes,
beats & phrases
I kick slick shit like
a natural born mule
gone mad underneath
the swelterin' heat
of the hellish southern sun
o' yeah
'cause you know
that I know
that you know
that I know
that you know
I'm bad
bend/in notes & folks' pain

in/to a deep shade of indigo moods
anchored in the bitter/sweet mud
of my mississippi muse
like b.b. king sings
everybody wanna know why I sing the blues
but few people brave enough to
walk a mile in my shoes

Conversations

against the hardcore 4/4 backbeat
of wild & wicked ass rhythms of
deep blues sweaty funk & roots rock reggae
angels traverse the dark midnight sky
screaming as you & I engage in
a strained but polite conversation
on the dusty dance floor
our bodies winding as one with the syncopated
rhythms of the saints
as we nice it up bogle style
while precious mountains of
massive asses
move & groove in sync like an ocean
motions with waves
upon waves
   up/on waves
up/on waves of syncopated sounds
washing our bodies clean with the nirvana of a
serpentine fire
quenching our burning desire to be one with the drum

Moanin' Blues

without a kind word or a thanks or a please
the devil came in on me this evenin'
he arrived about a quarter to five
&
brought the pain to my soul
when he nailed that eviction notice
on my front door
this cross I bear
is nothin'
but a financial ball & chain
say
this ole cross I bear
is nothin' but a doggone
financial ball & chain
worryin' 'bout money
will drive a man insane
& I ain't crazy…
yet

Never Let the Devil Call the Tunes

never let the devil call the tunes
while you dance
the dance of life
never, ever, ever, ever, ever
dance for, with or near
that old evil devil
he'll have you walking
the back streets crying
with a red hot thong shoved up your ass,
a black micro-mini skirt wrapped
around your waist
& a tattoo on your upper right thigh
saying
love for sale
love for sale
love for sale…
& it's cheap
dirt cheap
cheaper than
your impoverished grandchildren's
computer generated nightmare/dreams
subliminally embedded in the videos
they play every day on BET
cheaper than the blood diamonds
washed in the tears of your ancestors
cheaper than the red pill
morpheus gave neo
cheaper than
the wages paid
to girls shaking their asses
on stage at centerfolds
cheaper than reparations never paid to

slaves who paved the roads
that led all the way to the white house
cheaper than mammy's sweet milk
suckled by children
who weren't her own
cheaper than black life in mississippi in the 1920s
1930s
1940s
1950s
1960s
1970s
1980s
1990s
shit right now nigga!
right this very minute a black life
is being wasted
done in
snuffed out
murked
murdered
killed by the hand of a white man
killed by a system that the white man built
killed by the hand of a black man whose mind has
been killed
by the system that the white man built
& all the while the world
keeps on turning
& changing
& turning
& changing

& all around the world
the devil plays
the same old song
i got nothin' but love
for you baby
i got nothin' but love…
for sale
love for sale
love for sale
love for sale
& it's cheap,
cheap
cheap

Jimi Diggin' Cats at the Wallflower Societal Ball

it was a helluva hullabaloo
we sang the long black song
all doggone night
our fevered voices high
pitched a wang dang doodle
so strong till
sanity didn't bother
knocking on our door
only joy, gin and fish belly's
blues could do the do
for us
somewhere up in heaven
billions upon billions upon billions of
light years away from the sun
jimi sits on a cloud
of cosmic mushroom smoke screaming
like a dirty old man locked
in a house full of whores or
horrors
(i can never tell which is which)
his stratocaster fine-tuned in misery's
rock of ages
plays an electrified soulful twang tie-dyed
in sanctified west african rhythms
embedded with cryptic lyrics
looking
for the voodooo chile in us all
but we failed to see the light

'cross town the traffic's getting heavy
into jimi's jams
but the joes can't decipher
the code
see
this be
some heavy
      heavy
      heavy
doo doo dada
the kinda mumbo jumbo magic ish
reed kicked
after the big yellow radio
broke down
on a flight to canada
you can see freedom
forever following
the north star

Sankofa
(for Cassandra Wilson)

Oh Sankofa, high on the Heavens you soar / My soul is soon
to follow you, back to yesterday's moon...

we are both
embattled & bloody
like the sea that carried
our bruised & beloved
brothers & sisters
ancestors
raped & battered
fore parents
beaten & bludgeoned
bloody & blue
attracting a trail of famished
demons
sharks who eagerly devour
the beauty of our defiant black flesh
growing fat off the
seeds we sow in toil and turmoil
but like shine
our souls
still swim on
on through
the reign of the lash
laced with crimson & sweat
on
through yarugu's noose

naked with sadistic homoerotic
bloodlust
on
through the brutal torture
& molestation of generations
still scraping off the hideous memory of sadistic
seamen
from the painful middle passage
on
through the immoral injustice of
black codification peonage
& de facto slavery
on
past the uneven weight of
the sharecropper's scale
on
past the long hot summer of '64
on
past the freedom rides
boycotts & sit-ins
on
past the miles we marched in Mississippi & Louisiana
          the beatings we took in Georgia & Alabama
pausing only to honor
the lives we lost along the way
remembering that we swim for them
as they swam for us
to be born again & again & again

Grandma

My Lawd, don't move that mountain, just give me the strength to climb…

grandma sits on her
wooden porch
rocking in her wicker chair
swaying back & forth
       back & forth
moaning her monday morning blues
into the hot thick mid-day air
oblivious to the
sweaty-faced white man from
city hall as he tries to explain
why she has to leave
this place…
her house…
her home…
the one she spent over forty years
chopping
picking
scraping
& bailing cotton
until there was no more cotton left
to chop
pick
scrape
  or
bail

& when the cotton
was all gone
grandma
went on
to clean white folks nasty ass houses
cook their funny tasting food
& wiped their children's snotty ass noses
even when it meant seeing her own
go without
saving the little left over
after she finished feeding
the family
dog
&
cats
all this just to pay the bills
"but mable"
said the man from city government
his sweaty face flushed from the heat
& frustration of dealing with a stubborn
old nigger woman who refused to be moved
from her place
the righteous space that she bought & paid for
with her blood, sweat, tears & years of thankless toil
"...the city really needs this land, see
they got something called eminent domain
they can take your house anytime they want to
& ain't nothin' you can do about it
absolutely nothing
now mable if you just make and X right here
I promise I'll get you a fair price
I promise"
but what of the sentimental value
what price will the city pay

to erase the memories of living
in what was once her house
what amount will soothe her aching soul
whenever her heart longs to be back home
& what amount will wipe away
the pain of being
raped repeatedly by a system that has
no justice for an old black woman whose
soul nurtured the very boy
whom they sent to steal her land
the same way his father stole
the sanctity of her virgin black body over 40 yrs. ago
now the boy is a low-level city employee
sent to rape her of the only thing that she can point to
outside of her battered body & her humanity & say she
truly owned
 how could he!
"it's my job mable
lord knows I hate it
but I gotta do my job"
& then he proceeded to rape her
one more time by
robbing her of the only thing she knew she owned
her home
her sweet & precious home
the thing that sheltered her tired aching body from the
stormy memories of her past

now grandma sits
on the concrete porch

of the government owned apartment complex
cooling her sweaty brow with a fan from
cook's funeral home
still moaning her special brand of blues
her eyes, iced over with old age & cataracts, spare her
the agony of seeing her only son's sixteen-year-old
daughter turn tricks for a lick
on the devil's dick
for the price of a
white powdered rock
sold by some sick soul in the street
the son of the man
who stole her land
& the grandson
of the man whole stole her body
now steals her granddaughter's dignity
killing her softly
with each lustful stroke

Word/Life

& on that holy day
when you, word you
came down in/to
the valley of
my life
your wide eyes
sippin' my soul …
& then i felt you and your eyes
drink/in my soul & i knew
everything's gonna be alright
word/life
everything's gonna be alright.

Black Logos

go 'head
you can scream
shout
if you want
ain't no shame
or indignity in it
blues
is more than
shade or hue or color
'round here
see
one good thing
'bout music
music
sweet soulful
black music
when it hits
you feel no pain
but there is pain
in each emotional
measure
made of notes
forged from Black folks'
oppression
& bent &/or slid
in/to a three chord structure
played from
the plantation fields to
the back alleyways
to cafés/juke joints
of american history

shoutin' encoded messages
to buckra &
the world
don't matter what y'all say
or do
to me and mine
i am
all in all
i am
immortal as the time
conceived in my mind
long before
angels were born and
the devil knew his name
or
your
spirit was made flesh
i am/i be
a man
amen
a/man

That Old Black Music

do ya dig da music daddy

does it make you wanna
jump shout scream
touch a lucky dream
or
reach for the moon maybe
baby I know what you mean
when you say you ain't never seen
touched tasted anything
like this before in your life
but it is your life's music
living giving taking spirit quaking
soul shaking the roof of the savoy
sugar shack & cotton club
with ancient voudoun spirit rhythm & rhyme
time for a new day of history making
revolutionary black magic motion
with malismatic mau mau movement
sliding into a deeper shade of blue/blackness
ah man
come on
listen to it
listen to it carefully/thoughtfully
tellin' it
tellin' it
tellin' it
tellin' it
tellin' it
tellin it like it was/ is
to be forever be black magic music

make it ragtime swing bop be-bop
jazz/ funk/rock fusion
destroying the optical illusion cast by a
bitches' brew
cooked in a melting pot full of black blood, flesh &
teeth
america's only indigenous music
came to her in chains
untimely ripped from the loving womb of mama
africa
& dragged across raging seas
to a stolen land run by savages
who count their profits while tapping
their toes to the blues/jazz beat
ignoring the message/meaning
as it cuts through false definition
screaming you
took me
stole me
chained me
but you cannot
contain me
cannot control me
cannot hold me back forever
i don't belong to you
i never have
& i never will
for I belong to the people
who belong to the land of sun burnt skin
o' ancient & modern black magic music makers

standing somewhere
on the cutting edge of tradition
preaching a blues/jazz/gospel
for all the world to hear
we have & will not forget you
your gut-bucket-get-lucky-on-a-unlucky monday
work songs
were/are the sweet soothing salve
of hope healing the wounds of the oppressed

New Jack Swinging
(For Kevin Powell)

so ya really
wanna know the 411
on why five-o always be
hawkin & stalkin
sweatin & threatenin
shakin & breakin
us down all the time
ya see we be comin off
kinda phat with that
crazy mad assed flava
rollin hard down
the blvd charged
with the energy
of a brand new sound/system
packed 12 inches
deep with speakers
blastin like a 9mm
going BANG
with a chunk of dat
oops upside ya head funk
boomin a song born of
blood & struggle
bubblin from the bottom
of the world's socio-economic ladder
yeah we rock the mic
right like age old
word warriors hurlin

black bullets of explodin truth
bouncin from brooklyn
to t-neck to the
boogie down bronx
to brixton to watts
to soweto
see we be
the beepers the boppers
the hipsters the hoppers
singin ready or not
here we come
one nation
under a seriously slammin groove
standin on the verge
of a black boot stomp
into the future
we have come
to deliver the words
& make them hurt

Birmingham Blues

black boy's muse
sings ancestral
blues all through
the land where big bull's dogs
bit in/to the meaty
memories of charred flesh
devouring all that
is left of dreams
shattered with the gnashing
of rabid dog's teeth

birmingham
i remember you
like yesterday's lost souls singing
melodies of pain
softly in my ear
like a scorned lover longing
to be held just once
more

A Sufferer's Dream

no more….
back-way bumba clot baldhead
politicians lying while sticking
the people with pen/knives of
piously poisoned justice
enslaving the many who be
serving the few who be
fighting for power
but know not the hour
of doom's lick shot
drop

BOOOOOOOOOOOM!!!!!

S   P   R   E   A   D   O   U   T

soon come
the ethereal silence
of a golden millennium
imagine us
marooned in the eye of
a tropical storm waiting
to be born a/new generation of
old souls wailing on the winds of
change
it ain't no/thang that we come
forward with this vibration shaking
up a nation of zombies rising from
their *sleepless slumber* singing

sun up to sundown
a picking dat cotton

sun up to sundown
a cuttin' dat cane

night after night
I be hopin' and a prayin'

no mo auction block fo' me....
no more auction block for me
see we been trodding on the winepress
too much
too long
rebel toussaint
rebel martin
rebel malcolm
rebel nat
rebel denmark
rebel sojourner
rebel harriet
rebel marcus
rebel nandi
rebel boukman
rebel patrice
rebel for the sake of those
souls named & unnamed
known & unknown
whose bones
remain lost at the bottom
of a bitter and bloody sea

let our struggle forever be
a victorious libation
to their holy memory
a bile & bitter reminder
to whomever it may concern
that black blood don't come
as cheap as the wine flowing down
the destitute throats of those
whose souls still bear the scars of
ancestral oppression staggering up/town
looking for dirt roads on paved
city streets where flickering lights
of cracked pipes ignite their brains
with each breath
a darkened death in/hell
smothering them like black kittens in a white oven
come on and rise/up ye mighty people
more than sand
more than sea
more than numbers we are the real world
in ways more wonderful than 7
selah

Fly Fly Blackbird

it was me who
heard the blackbird
say that
the word is the way
the way is the word
sacred song sung
some
chant psalms so calm
it shakes the faith of
the faithful
whose blood spill filled
the pristine streets
of philistines who dream
of being philosopher/kings
of rhythm/less swing
                    please
don't sing me no mocking bird blues
don't play me no copycat jazz
i
  have
      heard
            e-
                nuff already……..she/it!

Part 2

Spirit/Word/Flame

Native Tongue

o eshu
why do you
mock me
for being a caged bird
singing the blues
sanctified by the moves
I use to
get through to you
I
drink rum
I
beat drum
I
go/come
dance in/trance
jerk & jerk
until
until
it hurts & hurts
but no matter what
I try
no/thing works
guess
toubob's tongues
won't run the voodoo
down like you do
eh eshu

Equestrian Death

old men
from days gone by
sit
at the end of a
dark & narrow
road
beating a dead horse
in the twilight sun
their blood boils
to a hundred degrees
celsius
while their hearts beat
to the theme song of
good times & happy days
but the carcass
will not rise
will not move
will not breathe
will not ease
on down the road
to nowhere
no matter what
or how many times
the men wail or wield
their whips & chains
pain & suffering
no longer afflict
the beast of burden
it will not be moved
nor will it die
it simply lies there

& suffers the ungodly pain
like a colt
being wielded to slaughter
there is no sound
except that of the
whip creasing the
animal's bloody flesh

old men
stone-faced and grim
swing their limbs
while singing their hymns
of battle
bones of the dead they rattle
as they beat the poor like cattle
hedging their bets
on just how long
these animals will last
how much more they will take
before they quietly expire
they're waging a fool's bet
as their beasts of burden
soon become
their feast of famine
cause every goodbye
ain't gone
every closed eye
ain't shut
& even the dead
       the dead

the dead
and unduly departed
can rise again

Et Tu Faith

big mama told me
to beware of wolves
dressed in sheep's clothing
said it was bad, bad bad
medicine
never good for the sickness
that plagues the soul of infants
much less a nation
stumbling in the darkness
of decadence and decay
"woe to the Shepherds who
scatter my flock" Jesus spoke
now he weeps
as lambs are openly led
to slaughter
their loving eyes forever watching
God saying et tu Jesus

Signifying on a Sadducee
(For Pat Robertson & His Ilk)

preacher pat
didn't yo mama tell you that
God don't like ugly
never has
never will
hence the reason
i suspect he don't like
hypocritical
cross-bearing
bible-thumping
holier-than-thou
theocratic
neo-conservative
bastards
like you

Orgy of Sin

the devil & dow jones
are throwing a party
an unsanctified soiree'
of unbridled bloodletting
allowing every unclean fiend
entrance into this unholy alliance
of pimps & tricks
including but not limited to
the whore of babylon
the wife of bath
the demonic ghost of j.p. morgan
andrew carnegie
nelson rockefeller
& all the cock-teasing sluts on wall street
rhythmically writhing in unchecked
government-sanctioned greed
climaxing into an orgy of
fiscal irresponsibility
leaving the middleclass
meek
mild
& mindless
without shoes to shod their blistering feet
or hope to keep them alive
stripped to their asses
& strapped for cash
with neither a pot to piss in
or a window

to throw it/up out of
even the dreams america gave them
have been repossessed
yet & still their bloodshot eyes continue
to move rapidly back and forth
as they lie asleep in the wet spot
of what was once their beloved country
only to wake to a neo-feudalistic world
without borders run by a small cabal
of corporate psychopaths hell bent on
stealing every ounce of gold
in their soul
for this
and this reason only
there can be no love song sung
for capitalism
no poetry pining for the glory days
of a free market economic beast
only funeral dirges and
battle hymns hummed
at the very top
of our defiant lungs echoing
poor though we may be
we will not tuck tail
& haul ass
just so the gluttonous elite
can feel secure in their cause
no
no
no our suffering
must be loud
it must be strong
and it must be heard

long after the flesh
from our bleeding carcass has been stripped
& cannibalized
the spirit from the marrow
of our broken bones
shall plague the darkness
of their sick souls
like a swarm of locusts in the dead
of an egyptian night
they shall be consumed

Haikus to the Sun

1
sun comes from the east
spraying yellow rays for all
who seek its love light

2
ah man ra sees all
who live, laugh, love, cry & die
beneath its bright warmth

3
good bad or ugly
no living creature can hide
nor darkness exist

4
without light of life
deeming it all possible
there will be no light

5
all souls seek solar
to bask and dance in its
abundance of life-giving

6
what a joy to see
the rising of ra again
thank god I still live

The Definition of Greed

these enemies we fight
are not imaginary
they ain't spooks
or haints
or ghosts
or goblins
or things that go bump
in the dark of night
nor are they alien clowns from outer space
swooping down in pimped-out flying saucers
to lord over us
like tyrants in a sci-fi movie
(huh, we should be so lucky)
no, these people
are real human beings
possessed by a spirit so wicked
so evil
so fiendishly diabolical
it could only come from
satan himself....

greed
is the insatiable psychopathic need to have and control
people, places...
things they know doggone well
they can't ever own
greed
is a crafty dollar

a seedy snake
& a bishop gone wrong
leaning in the ever lustful arms
of young nubile boys
whose tithes were taken
along with their innocence
praying for pie in the sky
while birds and rich folks flew
right on by
greed
is the chunky monkey on
the fat backs of capital
it is the jones gnawing at the underbelly
of corporate thugs called CEOs
who peddle poison
to the people by the scores
turning them out into
whores of consumption
(nothing sublime or subtle about it)

greed
is a gorilla pimp on steroids
pushing dope, dreams and derivatives
down the virgin throats of
joe the coach potato plumber
the arm chair conservative
who sipped the kool-aide
as though it were a six pack
of premium suds

greed
is the wicked cabal of neanderthals
that tea bagged the dreams
of suburban America

with nuts nastier than
the army of homeowners
left homeless in the wake
of the great wall street land-rush
oklahoma where the wind comes rushing down the plains
i imagine
we all feel like indians now
victims of financial saber rattling
whose dismal destiny was manifested
with the stroke of a banker's pen
like anthony bourdain, they'll
have no reservations when they discover
that the country/club
they thought they owned
actually owns them

greed
is a sin seven times deadlier than
unprotected AIDS infected sex
with sara paylin nailing the nation
to the flaming cross of free market
supply side economics
while george bush, dick cheney & companies
piss on the very ideal of a democratic republic
chanting
this land was never yours
this land was never yours
       was never yours
       was never ever ever yours

Apocalypto

these are the days that lead
up to the worst years of your life
the kind of times when men
would rather die than breathe
another stinking breath of air
punctuated with the perfume
of napalm and decayed flesh
remember them, america?
they are your children
the bright eyed youth
you sent to slaughter charlie
in vietnam
saddam in iraq
or al qaeda in afghanistan
the lost boys who wander
the wilderness of our history
wondering why
but for you the answer only
begs the question why not
the crows will eventually come home
to roost in the rot that you have all but created
give or take an unseen hand or two that
hides in the wretched shadows of your
wicked smile from which blood and lies flow
effortlessly as though you were born to do this
and nothing more
in these times when disaster lurks like darkness
on every street and death resides around every other
corner
your myopic vision as blurry and dismal as it is for the
world

will eventually fail you and all who follow in your staggering
footsteps that lead up to the fruition of doom
where will you go when the rabbit hole you run to
is filled with the bloody entrails of children you ordered
slaughtered in the name of a democracy that you knew
never really existed

2008 Post Election Analysis
(A Black Perspective)

a rock
to bash my head
a tree
to hang my neck
a river
to hide the body
400 years of slavery
share cropping
segregation
genocide & lynching
1 black president....
you do the math

I Dream of Jesus

last night i dreamed
i saw jesus pimp/strolling
peacock proud down crenshaw blvd
looking for lost souls
in the concrete valley of the damned

for 40 days and 40 nights
the son of man sought souls
in south central l.a.
home of the body bag, the bloods, the crips, the pigs
and the inner city blues
only to find shell shocked soldiers
raging over the rock of cocaine

last night i swear i saw jesus
dressed in black khakis, cracking a 40
and shooting the dozens while
hanging with all the homies in the hood
just cold kicking it
things were cool until some fool
lost his cool and shot another
jesus tried to save the brother
but couldn't
that's when all hell broke loose
tempers started flaring
gats got cracked
caps started popping
and niggas started dropping

like flies
the body count read:
12 injured,
3 dead,
crucified on the cross
of ghetto life

Breaking Between Two Worlds
(Jesus at the Crossroads)

& it came to pass
that the son of man
was called down to
the crossroads
where the loa of
the dead and
the spirit of the undead
meet in the sweet
by and by to try
& test the cool
of those who dare
to walk the walk
of the crossroad way
& break
between the beats of
mortals & gods
seek/in the holiness
of wisdom past
& wisdom present
embodied in the
orishas of that
old time religion

yeah jesus went
down to the old
rugged cross-
road to dance between

two worlds
his holy body breaking
to the beat of a music
loud enough to shake awake
the black saints of old
marching onward
like majestic warriors
chanting
in/to the hot dark delta night
(loa legba, loa legba, loa lega)
may the circle
be unbroken
by and by lord
by and by
& all the while
eshu watches the waning of the west
& elegba look longingly
to the east
admonishing jesus
to seek ye first
the holy kingdom
of ashe'
& all other wisdom
will be added on/in/to you
yo son of man
the choice is yours
you can get with this
or you can get with that

Hoodoo Poem

i say eshu
do not undo me
but do undo
the hoodoo done to me
by those foes who oppose
the flow of ashe'
from the next child
on to the next child
on to the next child
on to the next child
on to the next
stop
swinging redlight blinking
at the crossroad
an old man's grinding his organ
telling tales riddled with
too many meanings
as the loas/lords keep laughing
while I sit and wait for my fate
to be told in tongues
stranger than my own
wishing it was me who held
the key that fits
the lock of this most sacred
language/text
yet it is she/he who speaks this newspeak
based in old tales that wail
like a red rooster crowing

monday morning blues live
on a sad/day night
it's mama zulie stroking my
cock with the moistness
of her deep sour/sweet black soul
whispering wisdom is the ultimate orgasm
uh good god
can i get a witness
yeah
can i get some
well
if not can you at least teach me
to read the kola nut shells before
they come
to get you
stop
listen
to the beatbox/voice
of the sacred talking drum
hear the words
feel the feeling
let the rhythm reveal
& repeal
the smoke
that choked
the first fire within
o' say do you know she/he who
remembers the time
              the place
the words and ways of old
if so yo
tell 'em to go &
break the death code of slithering silence

tell 'em to
rock the mumbo jumbo so the humble can rumble
with that uncle in the jungle
tell 'em to
clear the air with ions of feeling tones
& while you're at it
tell 'em to kick in a couple of deep moans
so the spirit/bones of our ancestors
can rise and shine one mo' time
letting the good loas watch between me
& thee
until we meet again
amen

Swing Hamma Swing

o' nobody knows how
ole john henry
really feels
woke up this morning
kissing nine pounds
of steel sing

swing hamma swing
hamma swing swing swing
swing hamma swing
hamma swing swing swing

o' nobody really knows
what today may bring
john henry and ogun
versus the man
and his machine so sing

swing hamma swing
hamma swing swing swing
swing hamma swing
hamma swing swing swing

ya see I's chained
to this gang that makes me
work for free
they couldn't take my soul
so they stole my body
sing

swing hamma swing
hamma swing swing swing
swing hamma swing
hamma swing swing swing

but I's a man
with a will of steel
I got what it takes
to fill the bill
& if I don't get justice
ole shango will

swing hamma swing
hamma swing swing swing
swing hamma swing
hamma swing swing swing

Libations
> (for Virgia Brocks-Shedd)

for you sweet black
woman of southern
roads whose dusty
feet walked the
city streets
as proud as can be
seeking the sweet
wine of wisdom from the
nectar of life's blues
as you moved throughout
your life on this plane
touching all with
the holiness of your vision
rooted in ancestral spirit of old
weaving a web of magic words
warmly wrapped in the sweetness of your soul

for you mother of earth
grandest daughter of sacred
southern dust
whose shadow forever embraced the ground
everyday in the radiant light
of your life
leading me on back to the path
where southern roads
met piney woods
& piney woods met tougaloo
& tougaloo
met you

for you o great grand daughter
of jubilee I offer thee
this humble libation of words
as my tribute to you
whose name I will intone
for lifetimes to come
say
may the sweet water of your words
forever flow from the mouths
of backwood southern babes
in praise of you
my mississippi mama

Rockstar Jesus

& on the third night
jesus wept
his tears a bittersweet
mixture of blood and sweat
flowed like the river nile
staining the urban concrete
streets crimson red
with the anguish of his undying love
screaming:
    "father o' father why
     have you forsaken them
     in their hour of dire need"
but there was no answer
coming from the cool cruel streets
of south central
only the faint sound of
gunshots, screams and broken glass
echoing throughout the city
so the sun of man turned his back
on the night and took a hit
from the glass pipe

& now jesus is a rockstar touring the ho'-stroll
looking for a strawberry toss-up
to wash his weary feet
before his next craving
comes crashing down
like the wailing walls
of jericho

South Central Olympics

it's happy hour
here on the d-day
of decision for
the masses of
south central
los angeles and
the son of man
stands still
at the blazing edge of night
his hand tightly
clutching
a molotov cocktail
shouting
"no justice no peace
  no peace no justice!
  yo yall, it's on
strike a match and
let the flames begin"

Jesus on the RTD

yesterday
while riding the rtd
jesus christ appeared to me
suddenly
like the physical manifestation
of my third eye
apparently he was
still looking for lost souls
to feed
the secret words of sacred power

all alone the son of man sat
on a seat next to the
window side
his bloodshot eyes forever fixed on
the direction of the rising sun
singing:
        "to the east my brother
          to the east..."
but few people caught the wisdom
of his holy words
because few people cared
enough to hear
or either they were too scared
to listen
so the savior
having been rejected for a third time
stepped off at the next stop
to cast his pearls elsewhere

Speak No Evil

do not speak to me of truth
do not tell me tall tales of
wealth & prosperity
tell me the truth
and you can spare me
the tired lecture
about america's moral
obligation to the free world
here in the belly of the beast
where the great wicked
whore of babylon
speaks no truth
but does much evil
no
no
no
I have had it up to here
with your filthy lies
my cup runneth over
spilling blood, blood
omnipotent blood
on the rocky road to freedom

.

www.ingramcontent.com/pod-product-compliance
Lightning Source LLC
Chambersburg PA
CBHW031006090426
42737CB00008B/704